Heart of a Galaxy

Mari Bolte

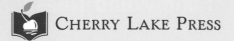

CHERRY LAKE PRESS

Published in the United States of America by Cherry Lake Publishing Group
Ann Arbor, Michigan
www.cherrylakepublishing.com

Reading Adviser: Beth Walker Gambro, MS, Ed., Reading Consultant, Yorkville, IL
Content Adviser: Robert S. Kowalczyk, MS, Physics, Systems Engineer (Retired) at the NASA Jet Propulsion Laboratory

Photo Credits: page 1: © ESA/Webb, NASA & CSA, J. Lee and the PHANGS-JWST Team. / flickr.com; page 5: © Acknowledgement: J. Schmidt / Wikimedia; page 6: © NASA/JPL-Caltech/ESO/R. Hurt / Shutterstock; page 9: © muratart / Getty Images; page 10: © Alexandr Yurtchenko / esawebb.org; page 12: © ESA/Webb, NASA & CSA, J. Lee and the PHANGS-JWST Team. / nasa.gov; page 15: © Acknowledgement: J. Schmidt / esahubble.org; page 16: © NASA / flickr.com; page 19: © ESA/Hubble & NASA, J. Lee and the PHANGS-HST Team / nasa.gov; page 20: © Acknowledgement: Judy Schmidt (Geckzilla) / esahubble.org; page 22: © Science - NASA, ESA, CSA, and J. Lee (NOIRLab). Image processing - A. Pagan (STScI) / flickr.com; page 25: © NASA, ESA, CSA, and STScI / nasa.gov; page 26: © ESA/Hubble & NASA, R. Chandar / flickr.com

Cherry Lake Press is an imprint of Cherry Lake Publishing Group.

Library of Congress Cataloging-in-Publication Data
Library of Congress Cataloging-in-Publication Data has been filed and is available at catalog.loc.gov.

ISBN 9781668938355 Lib.

Cherry Lake Publishing Group would like to acknowledge the work of the Partnership for 21st Century Learning, a Network of Battelle for Kids. Please visit Battelle for Kids online for more information.

Note from publisher: Websites change regularly, and their future contents are outside of our control. Supervise children when conducting any recommended online searches for extended learning opportunities.

Printed in the United States of America

Mari Bolte is an author and editor of children's books in every subject imaginable. She hopes the next generation sets their sights on the sky and beyond. Never stop the love of learning!

CONTENTS

CHAPTER 1

Gaze into the Galaxies

In the darkness of space, there spins a shining galaxy. Its gases, dust, stars, and planets are all bound together by gravity. The largest galaxies have a supermassive **black hole** at the center. No two galaxies are the same. The *James Webb Space Telescope* is helping scientists uncover the mystery at the heart of each one.

Earth is part of the Milky Way Galaxy. It has more than 100 billion stars and 100 billion planets. The galaxy is 100,000 **light-years** from one end to the other. Our solar system is about halfway between the center and the outside of the Milky Way. What if it was possible to travel at the speed of light? That is 186,000 miles (300,000

We are here

Our solar system is located on a part of the Milky Way called the Orion Spur.

kilometers) per second. It would still take us 25,000 light-years to get to the heart of the Milky Way.

The *James Webb Space Telescope* left Earth in December 2021. It reached its final destination on January 24, 2022. Its scientific tools have been hard at work. The telescope has sent back images of outer space trillions of miles away. Those pictures have peered into the very heart of strange and wondrous galaxies.

Webb Telescope Facts

The *James Webb* is the LARGEST AND MOST POWERFUL space telescope ever.

After leaving Earth's atmosphere, it traveled through space at 720 MILES (1,160 KM) PER HOUR.

Webb is orbiting our Sun approximately 1 MILLION MILES (1.6 MILLION KM) from Earth.

CHAPTER 2

Heart of the Phantom Galaxy

If you live in the Northern Hemisphere, take a look at the night sky between October and December. You may see the constellation Pisces. If you could look 32 million light-years beyond that, you would be able to see M74. This is also known as the Phantom Galaxy.

Like the Milky Way, the Phantom Galaxy is in the shape of a spiral. It is known as a grand design spiral. It has large, well-defined arms. They circle out from the center. Only 10 percent of all known galaxies are grand designs. They are usually the brightest in the universe. Other types of galaxies are barred spiral, **elliptical**, and irregular.

The center of the Phantom Galaxy is a dense **nuclear** star cluster. These clusters are often found in galaxies like ours.

Pisces is one of the largest constellations in the nighttime sky. It was first introduced by Claudius Ptolemy, a Greek astronomer, in the 2nd century CE.

Studying nuclear star clusters can help scientists understand how galaxies are formed.

Scientists have been looking at the Phantom Galaxy for a long time. It can be seen from Earth using small telescopes. French astronomer Pierre Méchain first discovered it in 1780. The *Hubble Space Telescope* was launched more than 200 years later in 1990. It orbits Earth. *Hubble* took images of the Phantom Galaxy in 2007. In 2022, the *James Webb Space Telescope* took the most detailed photos to date.

Like the Milky Way, the Phantom Galaxy is made from around 100 BILLION stars.

The Phantom Galaxy faces the Milky Way nearly head-on. This makes it easier to see its SPIRAL SHAPE from Earth.

Phantom Galaxy Facts

Webb's cameras captured never-before-seen threads coming off the Phantom Galaxy's SPIRAL ARMS. Each delicate strand is made of gas and dust.

While *Hubble* was only supposed to run for 15 years, it has been in operation for over 30.

One of *Webb*'s first missions was to take photos of the Phantom Galaxy. They were compared to similar photos from the *Hubble Space Telescope*. *Webb* is not a replacement for *Hubble*. They use different light **wavelengths** to create images.

Everything gives off **electromagnetic radiation**. The human eye can see a small amount of radiation. It is called the visible light spectrum. *Hubble* uses the visible light spectrum. It also uses **ultraviolet** (UV) light. UV light has shorter wavelengths. *Webb* uses **infrared** and near-infrared wavelengths to look at stars. These wavelengths are longer than the visible light spectrum. *Webb* can also detect some visible light, but it does not use UV light.

As light travels across space, it stretches. This is because of the expansion of the universe. The stretching increases its wavelength. Light waves that start on the visible spectrum stretch closer and into infrared. *Hubble* orbits Earth just above the planet's atmosphere. It can see objects around 13.4 billion light-years away. *Webb* can see even farther than that because of its infrared cameras. When we see things that far away, we are actually seeing into the past.

Hubble and *Webb* have taken pictures of the same things. However, *Webb* can see farther back in time. It can show us galaxies in their younger form.

HISTORY OF *HUBBLE*

The views from the ground have amazed scientists since 1609. It wasn't until the 1940s that Lyman Spitzer threw out the idea of sending a telescope into space. Thirty years later, the European Space Agency (ESA) and the National Aeronautics and Space Administration (NASA) paired up. They started work on the first space telescope. It was called *Hubble*.

The *Hubble Space Telescope* was launched on April 25, 1990. Its orbit is over 300 miles (480 km) above Earth. On May 20th of that year, it sent back its first image. It was an unimpressive sight. The star HD96755 is 1,300 light-years away. Through *Hubble*'s lens, it appeared as white dots in a fuzzy gray sky. But this was just a teaser for what was to come. *Hubble*'s photos continued to improve.

CHAPTER 3

The Great Barred Spiral Galaxy

The Phantom Galaxy is only one of the 19 galaxies *Webb* will target during its mission. NGC 1365 is another. Viewers in the Southern Hemisphere might see the constellation of Fornax between October and December. Fifty-six million light-years in that direction is NGC 1365. This is also known as the Great Barred Spiral Galaxy.

At the center of NGC 1365 lies a black hole. It is small compared to some. But its **mass** is great. It is more than 2 million times more massive than our Sun. The black hole spins at nearly the speed of light. No other black hole has been measured with such accuracy. Its high rate of speed means dust, gas, and other matter are being pulled in from one direction.

Hubble photographed NGC 1365 in 2020. Black holes at the center of galaxies compress and heat material with so much force that they glow brightly across wavelengths.

Scientists have found that the more stars a galaxy has, the faster it makes new ones. They may have more material to make new stars. They may be better at making them. The truth is that nobody knows yet. But with *Webb*'s help, more of NGC 1365's secrets will be revealed.

NGC 1365 is TWICE AS LARGE as the Milky Way. Its black hole is believed to be 2 million miles (3.2 million km) wide.

NGC 1365 Facts

NGC 1365 has wide arms called bars that stretch out to make an S shape. One is longer than the other.

Other space telescopes have had LIMITED VIEWS of the smaller bar because of dust in the way.

CHAPTER 4

Bursting with Stars

In October 2022, *Webb* captured an amazing sight. Around 270 million light-years away, a collision took place. The galaxies IC 1623 A and B are merging. The place where they meet is called a starburst. Here, stars are being created at an amazing rate. The supermassive black hole may have an effect on local galaxies.

Hubble and other space telescopes have taken pictures of the galaxies. But the area is full of space dust. This makes it hard for shorter wavelengths to reach what's happening inside. Using infrared, scientists can look past the dust. *Webb* can pick up the intense infrared rays coming off of the merging galaxies.

WHAT IS COSMIC DUST?

Outer space is a dusty place. Cosmic dust is made up of tiny **particles** of matter. They float around between the stars and planets. The dust includes heavy elements like carbon, iron, and oxygen. It's different from the dust in your house. Cosmic dust is more like a heavy cloud with solid bits floating along with it. For years, scientists didn't know how it was made or where it came from. Then in 2011, a star exploded. This is called a supernova. Scientists were able to see a huge amount of cosmic dust coming from it. The dust cloud was freezing cold. It reached temperatures of around −429 to −416 degrees Fahrenheit (−256 to −249 degrees Celsius). The explosion made 10,000 times more dust than expected.

When two massive black holes merge, they send out huge amounts of energy. This image of IC 1623 was taken by *Hubble* on June 21, 2021.

IC 1623 is creating a starburst galaxy. These are galaxies that form stars at a very fast rate. Dust and gas mix to create them. But *Webb* can see through that dust. That's what makes IC 1623 shine so bright through *Webb*'s lens.

Post-starburst galaxies were common back when the universe was first formed. They are less common now. The nearest examples are millions of light-years away. *Webb*'s research could help scientists learn more about how galaxies change. This can tell them more about our Milky Way Galaxy and its future.

Eyes in the Sky

Different telescopes are designed to see different things. *Hubble* and *Webb* are showing us that pictures of the same things look different. The more eyes in the sky, the more we can learn! The next space telescope will be the *Nancy Grace Roman Space Telescope*.

	Hubble	Webb	Roman
Launch Date	April 24, 1990	December 25, 2021	May 2027
Telescope Size	7.9 feet (2.4 meters)	21 feet (6.4 m)	7.9 feet (2.4 m)
Location	332 miles (534 km) from Earth; orbits Earth	1 million miles (1.6 million km) from Earth; orbits the Sun	1 million miles (1.6 million km) from Earth; the same location as *Webb*
Mission	Take high-resolution observations to open new windows into planets, stars, and galaxies.	Study every phase in the history of our universe, while building on *Hubble*'s discoveries.	Look for **dark energy**, **dark matter**, and **exoplanets**, while exploring using infrared technology.
Scientific Tools	6	4	2
Mission Duration	Originally 15 years; still active	5 to 10 years	5 years, plus 5 potential additional years

IC 1623 Facts

IC 1623 is creating new stars 20 TIMES FASTER than the Milky Way.

Some starburst galaxies can make new stars HUNDREDS OF TIMES FASTER.

Studying STARBURST GALAXIES can help scientists understand how galaxies evolve.

CHAPTER 5

Pearls Above

Webb is helping researchers across the spectrum of space science. NASA, the ESA, and the Canadian Space Agency (CSA) worked together to build it. They each help oversee the telescope's operation.

Hundreds of other companies added their own pieces. Thousands of scientists, engineers, and technicians joined in. Together, 14 countries all gave time and money to the project's success. Scientists from around the world work together. They study the images *Webb* sends back to Earth. These scientists have started many programs.

One of those programs is called PEARLS. That stands for the Prime **Extragalactic** Areas for **Reionization** and Lensing Science. Its goal is to study how galaxies are born and formed. In December 2022, *Webb* captured a section of the sky with its Near-Infrared Camera (NIRCam).

NIRCam also saw two different types of hydrogen in NGC 346, revealing essential building blocks of star and planet formation. The gases are shown in pink and orange.

This camera can detect light from early stars and young galaxies just forming. PEARLS studied the photos and made a discovery. There was evidence of giant black holes at the center of some of the earliest galaxies. The team was also able to see faint red dots. These are distant galaxies that date back to a few hundred million years after the Big Bang.

NIRCam Facts

Many images are combined to create a MOSAIC. Imagine taking multiple pictures of the same group of people, then combining them into a single photo so nobody is blurry.

Webb's NIRCam can see things BILLIONS OF LIGHT-YEARS away. This means it can observe stars and galaxies as they appeared 13.6 billion years ago.

NIRCam has 10 DETECTORS that use different short and long wavelengths.

The first PEARLS images were taken looking toward the constellation Draco. The images were enhanced with images from *Hubble*. "I was blown away by the first PEARLS images," said Rolf Jansen, a research scientist. "I can see streams, tails, shells, and halos of stars in their outskirts, the leftovers of building blocks."

Most of the objects in the PEARLS image, on the previous spread, are invisible to the human eye. The cameras on *Webb* make them visible. The larger galaxies are 9 billion years old. In the image, we see them as they were 4.6 billion years ago.

During that time, the universe was more active. Galaxies were being born. Others collided. The brightest spots in the image are galaxies with supermassive black holes at their center. *Webb* can see their infrared light. It glitters like diamonds across the night sky.

NEVER STOPPING, ALWAYS MOVING

You may already know that the planet beneath your feet is moving. Earth's spin makes day and night. At the same time, it rotates around the Sun. But did you know that the Sun, the solar system, and even the galaxy are also in constant motion? When dinosaurs roamed Earth millions of years ago, our solar system was on the opposite side of the Milky Way.

The way things move through space depends on the gravities of the other galaxies around them. The Milky Way and around 100,000 nearby galaxies are being pulled toward a huge concentration of matter. Scientists call it the Great Attractor. The Milky Way is being pulled at 1.3 million miles (2 million km) per hour.

The movement can be tracked over time. *Hubble* has kept track of our nearest neighbor, the Andromeda Galaxy. It is around 2.5 million light-years away. *Hubble* confirmed it will eventually collide with the Milky Way. Don't worry, though. That won't happen for 4.5 billion more years. Scientists have also been able to track the motions of another 10,000 galaxies!

Activity

Connect to STEAM: Art

Connect to the "A" in STEAM by putting your art skills to the test. *Webb* takes many different shots of the same thing. Then it layers the photos together. Borrow that idea by coloring the same scene onto several different layers of see-through paper.

MATERIALS NEEDED

- chalk or chalk pastels
- a picture from the *James Webb Space Telescope*
- blue or black construction paper
- masking tape
- four pieces of transparent vellum paper
- colored pencils
- fine-tipped markers

1. Use the chalk to replicate the broader, more colorful swirls in the *Webb* picture onto the construction paper. Set aside.

2. Tape down the *Webb* picture. Then set a piece of vellum paper over the top. Use colored pencils and markers to draw details on the vellum paper.

3. Set a second sheet of vellum paper on top. Tape them together at one end. Then set the vellum papers back onto the night sky photo. Add even more artistic details. Repeat with two more pieces of vellum paper.

4. When you've finished, you should have four pieces of vellum paper taped together like a book. Set the book on top of the construction paper and tape them together.

5. Do the colors of the construction paper shine through? If they need a boost, add more swirls of color on each piece of vellum paper. The more layers you add, the more intense the colors will be!

Find Out More

Books

Bolte, Mari. *Space Discoveries*. Ann Arbor, MI: Cherry Lake Publishing, 2022.

Collins, Ailynn. *Investigating the Milky Way and Other Galaxies with Velma*. North Mankato, MN: Capstone Press, 2023.

Hirsch, Rebecca E. *Stars and Galaxies in Action: An Augmented Reality Experience*. Minneapolis: Lerner Publications, 2020.

Space: A Visual Encyclopedia. New York: DK Publishing, 2020.

Online Resources to Search with an Adult

Britannica for Kids: *James Webb Space Telescope*

NASA Space Place: What Is a Galaxy?

NASA Space Place: What Is the *James Webb Space Telescope*?

TIME for Kids: Seeing into Space

Glossary

black hole (BLAK HOHL) an invisible area with gravity so strong that space objects and light cannot escape its pull

dark energy (DAARK EH-nuhr-jee) a force in space that is thought to work against gravity

dark matter (DAARK MA-tuhr) an invisible substance in space that is thought to affect gravity

electromagnetic radiation (ih-lek-troh-mag-NEH-tik ray-dee-AY-shuhn) a stream of both electric and magnetic energy that flows in a wavelike pattern

elliptical (ih-LIP-tik-uhl) oval-shaped

exoplanets (EK-soh-plah-nuhts) planets outside our solar system

extragalactic (ek-struh-guh-LAK-tik) outside the Milky Way Galaxy

infrared (in-fruh-RED) invisible light from beyond the red end of the visible light spectrum

light-years (LYTE-YEERZ) units of distance equal to how far light travels in 1 year—6 trillion miles (10 trillion km)

mass (MAS) how much material an object contains, giving it weight when influenced by gravity

nuclear (NOO-klee-uhr) having to do with the energy created when atoms are split apart

particles (PAHR-tih-kuhlz) very small, basic units of matter

reionization (ree-iye-uh-nuh-ZAY-shuhn) a phase in the early universe when unstable early stars are believed to have exploded and split atoms into electrically charged pieces called ions

ultraviolet (uhl-truh-VIE-luht) invisible light from beyond the violet end of the visible light spectrum

wavelengths (WAYV-lengths) measurements between one wave to another as energy flows through space in a wavelike pattern

Index